Cycling

Hazel Maskell

Illustrated by Mark Reihill

Designed by Helen Edmonds and Zoe Wray

Edited by Emily Bone   Cycling expert: Anna Magrath

Following a trail through caves in South Africa on a mountain bike

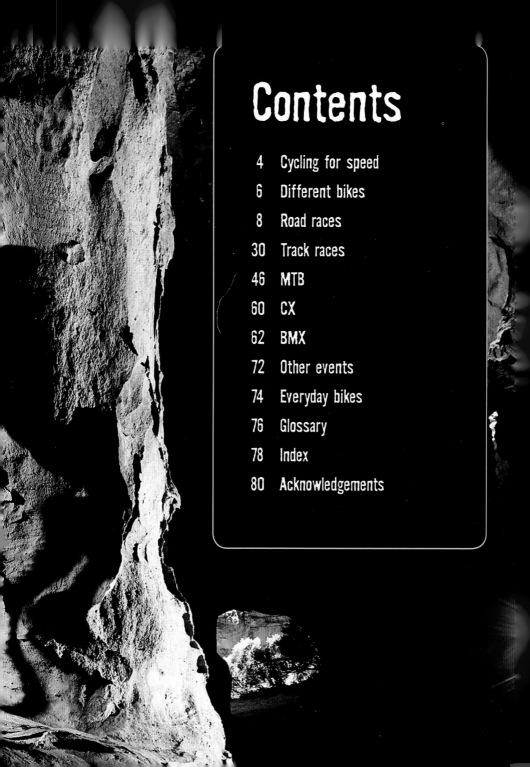

Contents

Cycling for speed

For over a hundred years, cycling has been an exciting way of covering distances at high speeds. Today, top cycling competitions vary from thrilling, fast-paced races to runs of amazing tricks and jumps.

These riders are competing in the Tour de France in 2014. In the stage shown here, which took place in northern England, racers cycled over 200km (124 miles). See pages 14-15 for more on the Tour de France.

Different bikes

Different bikes are designed for different types, or **disciplines**, of cycling. The four main disciplines of competitive cycling are track, road, mountain biking and BMX.

This photograph shows Scottish cyclist and six-time Olympic Games gold-medal winner Sir Chris Hoy in 2011. When Hoy was younger, he raced BMX bikes.

Held every four years, the Olympic Games are among the biggest sporting events in the world. They include events in all the main cycling disciplines.

Track bikes are built for speed. On these bikes, top riders can reach speeds of up to 80km/h (50mph).

BMX freestyle bikes are used for jumps and tricks. They have strong frames to withstand hard impacts, and wide wheels to help riders to balance.

These bikes often have modifications such as **pegs** on the wheels that help the rider to perform tricks.

Modern bikes			
Road bikes	**Track bikes**	**Mountain bikes**	**BMX bikes**
Great bikes for getting around on hard, even surfaces. See pages 20-21.	Very fast bikes used on very smooth surfaces. See page 34.	Rugged bikes for off-road riding. See page 48.	Small bikes, great for jumps, speed or tricks. See page 63.

Road races

Road races can be anything from short tests of speed, to spectacular long-distance events that last for weeks. The top road races are incredibly tough, and contested by teams of professionals.

This women's road race was part of the 2012 Olympic Games in London. For the Olympics, racers compete in national teams, and each country has its own team uniform.

These racers are all setting off together. This is called a **mass start**.

Helmets are shaped to cut through the air, which helps the racer to go faster. See page 10.

Skin-tight clothing, made of a stretchy, strong fabric

These are road bikes, with high-set seats. See pages 20-21 for more on road bikes.

Different road competitions

- **Time trials** are races against the clock. See pages 22-23.
- **Criteriums** are short races, usually an hour long. They are made up of laps around a closed section of road, often in a town or city.
- **Day races** take place around a circuit, or from one point to another. The longest is seven hours long.
- **Stage races** are long races, made up of a series of day races. They can go on for up to three weeks. See pages 12-17.

Most riders spend the race riding together in a pack called a **peloton**.

A **breakaway** is when a small group of riders escapes off the front of the peloton. If these riders manage to stay ahead, they will reach the finish first – so they often work together to keep their lead, even if they are on different teams.

Dutch rider Marianne Vos took the gold medal.

Racing teams

The best road racers belong to elite teams called **trade teams**, sponsored by businesses or companies who pay for equipment and training. In return, riders must follow their teams' strategies, even if it means giving up their own chances of winning to help a teammate to victory.

This racer is part of the Belkin Pro Cycling Team, one of 18 top-tier racing teams.

Pacelines and taking a pull

Moving forward on a bike involves pushing through the air. The way air pushes against a moving object is known as **air resistance**. The faster a rider goes, the more effort it takes. However, a team of riders can take turns doing the hard work of pushing through air, by riding in a line called a **paceline**.

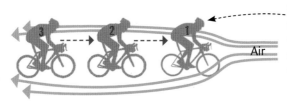

Rider 1 pushes aside air, creating an area behind called a **slipstream**. In the slipstream, there is less air resistance, so it takes up to 40% less effort for his teammates to pedal.

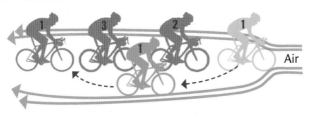

After a few minutes, rider 1 is tired, so he drops back. It's Rider 2's turn to **take a pull** (go at the front).

Racers must wear clothing that advertizes their main sponsors.

Team cars carry drinks and snacks, spare bikes, a mechanic, and someone who gives information and orders called a **directeur sportif** – the French for 'sporting director'. The world's main governing body for sports cycling, the UCI, was founded in France. Read more about the UCI on page 13.

At 2,757m (9,045ft) high, these Giro d'Italia competitors face snow and ice even in May as they ride along the Stelvio Pass, one of the highest roads in the Alps. Mountain stages are very tough, and only the very best cyclists are able to take the lead.

The Grand Tours

The Grand Tours are the three most famous road races – the **Giro d'Italia**, the **Vuelta a España** and the **Tour de France**. Held on new routes every year, they each take place over three weeks, and are made up of day races called **stages**. Each Tour is based in its home country, but may pass into other countries too.

Grand Tours statistics

- **Average total distance:** 3,000-4,000km (1,864-2,486 miles)
- **Average total winner's time:** 80-85 hours
- **Number of contestants:** usually 198 – made up of 22 teams of 9
- **Number of days:** 23 – made up of 21 racing days and 2 rest days
- **Number of stages:** 21 – which always include some stages through mountain ranges, and at least one time trial

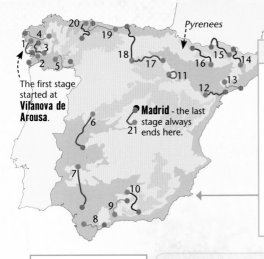

The first stage started at **Vilanova de Arousa**.

Pyrenees

Madrid - the last stage always ends here.

Vuelta a España

- **Country:** Spain
- **Month held:** September
- **Biggest mountain range:** the Pyrenees
- **Leader wears:** a red jersey
- **First held in:** 1935
- **Most wins:** Tony Rominger, Roberto Heras - 3 wins each

The 2013 route is shown.

Key

- ● Start point
- ◑ End point
- — Time trial
- — Flat stage
- — Moderate climb
- — Mountain stage
- ▦ Mountains
- ▦ Hilly land
- ▦ Flat land

Who oversees cycle races?

All big races are overseen by the **Union Cycliste Internationale**, based in Switzerland.

The UCI is a cycling body that awards points for wins, gives penalties, sets rules, and calculates world rankings. It also organizes some races directly – see pages 24-25.

Dolomites

Alps

The last stage ended in **Brescia**.

Stages 15 and 16 went into France.

Racers usually travel between stages on their team bus. Over longer distances, they may go by plane.

Rome

Apennines

The first stage was in **Naples**.

Giro d'Italia

- **Country:** Italy
- **Months held:** May-June
- **Biggest mountain range:** the Alps, including the Dolomites
- **Leader wears:** a pink jersey
- **First held in:** 1909
- **Most wins:** Alfredo Binda, Fausto Coppi, Eddy Merckx - 5 wins each

The 2013 route is shown. Stage 19 wasn't raced due to bad weather.

Jerseys

The Tour's leaders wear special jerseys. These are awarded after each stage result is announced, and then at the end given to the final winners.

Yellow jersey – worn by the **General Classification** leader (the racer with the fastest overall time over the stages)

Polka-dot jersey – worn by the **King of the Mountains** (the best climber, fastest going up mountain climbs)

Green jersey – worn by the **Points Classification** leader (the racer who has won the most points, for wins and intermediate sprints)

White jersey – awarded to the **Best Young Rider** (the best racer under 25). It's rare for these younger racers to win in other categories.

Only one cyclist has ever won the General Classification, Points and King of the Mountains jerseys in a single Tour de France. This was Belgian racer Eddy Merckx in 1969.

Route of the Tour de France

The Tour de France covers around 3,500km (2,175 miles) of roads every year, through towns and cities and up and down steep mountains. The route is lined by millions of spectators, cheering on the cyclists.

Tour de France 2013

The 2013 Tour was the 100th Tour de France. To celebrate the anniversary, the unusual decision was taken to hold the Tour entirely within France. Its route is shown below.

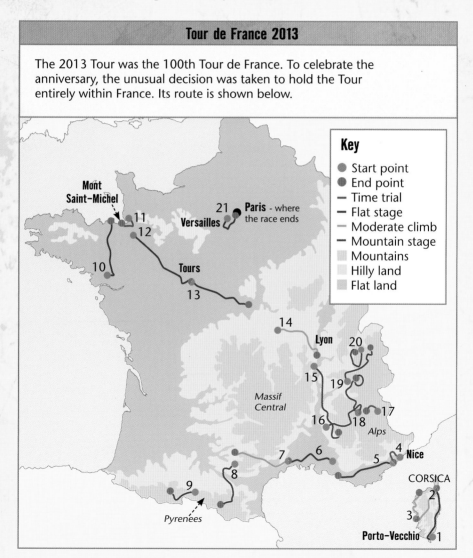

Key
- ● Start point
- ◑ End point
- — Time trial
- — Flat stage
- — Moderate climb
- ▬ Mountain stage
- ▨ Mountains
- ▨ Hilly land
- ▨ Flat land

Mont Saint-Michel

11
12
10
Tours
13

21 Versailles
Paris - where the race ends

14
Lyon
20
15
19
Massif Central
16
18 17
Alps

7 6
8
5 4 Nice
9
Pyrenees

CORSICA
2
3
Porto-Vecchio 1

The Tour de France

The Tour de France is the biggest cycling race in the world. Watched in 190 countries by over 100 million viewers, it sees racers compete for the leader's **maillot jaune** (yellow jersey).

Tour de France

- **Home country:** France
- **Months:** June-July
- **First held in:** 1903
- **Most wins:** Jacques Anquetil, Eddy Merckx, Bernard Hinault, Miguel Indurain – 5 wins each*

Flat stages: 170-220km (106-137 miles)

Racers usually ride in groups – the peloton or a breakaway. Most flat stages end in a dash to the finish in the final seconds, often won by a fast rider called a **sprinter** at speeds of over 65km/h (40mph).

Mountain stages: 140-200km (87-125 miles)

Tough, steep climbs break up the riders, as racers drop behind or race ahead. The best **climbers** can win by whole minutes.

The first racers to the **top of big climbs** win points that count towards the King of the Mountain classification. Lift the flap to learn more.

* Lance Armstrong once held 7 wins. But he was stripped of them all in 2012 after being found guilty of cheating, including taking drugs to improve his performance

Most stages include an **intermediate sprint line**. The first riders over it win points towards the points classification.
Lift the flap to learn more.

Time trials: 25–50km (15–31 miles) In time trial stages, all racers try to set the quickest time over a set stretch of road, either alone or as a team. See pages 22-23 for more about time trials.

Final finishing line

Since 1975, the last stage has ended at a famous avenue in Paris called the Champs Elysées.

The Alpe d'Huez road climbs up to 1,850m (6,070ft) over 13.8km (8.6 miles), and includes 21 sharp turns, known as **hairpin bends.**

Some spectators arrive hours or even days before the Tour arrives, to get into a good position to watch the race.

15a

Here you can see stage 18 of the 2013 Tour. The riders raced up a mountain climb known as **Alpe d'Huez** – then descended and climbed it again.

The rider in yellow has the fastest time over all the stages so far.

History of the Tour

Ever since the first contestants set off over 100 years ago, the Tour de France has been one of the most dramatic sporting events in the world. It has seen legendary clashes, bitter rivalries and breathtaking wins.

The 1964 Tour saw top racer Jacques Anquetil (left) race Raymond Poulidor, a cyclist popular with the crowds, for 10km (6 miles) uphill to keep the yellow jersey. Their elbow-to-elbow battle became legendary.

Poulidor finished ahead of Anquetil by seconds – but it was not enough to take over the lead. Anquetil went on to win the Tour.

The racers were followed closely by photographers, police, officials and team cars.

The first Tour de France

In 1902, journalist Géo Lefèvre had an idea to boost sales of the sports newspaper he worked for – organizing a new cycling race around France.

His editor, an avid cyclist called Henri Desgrange, agreed.

On July 1, 1903, 60 men set off from Paris, competing for a share of the 20,000 francs prize.

The leader wore a green armband.

There were only six stages, but they were more than twice as long as stages today. Even the fastest cyclists took nearly 18 hours to finish the longest stretches.

Pssssst

Winner, Maurice Garin

Riders used whatever tactics they could to win – even cheating. On one occasion, leaders threw glass bottles to puncture rivals' wheels.

Just 21 men made it across the finish line – cheered on by 20,000 fans. The Tour had been a huge success.

The Classics

The Classics are day races that take place in Europe every year. There are over a dozen, and most have been running for a long time – the first was held in 1892. The UCI uses some of the results to rank racers, so many top cyclists take part.

This photograph shows part of the 1967 Paris-Roubaix race. This Classic is famous for its stretches of cobbled road, called **pavé**.

The Monuments			
The Monuments are the five most famous Classics of all. Most routes vary each year, but they are always 250-300km (155-185 miles) long and last 6-7 hours.			
Name and nicknames	**When raced**	**First raced**	**Route description**
Milan–San Remo, Italy The Spring; the Classic of Classics	Mid-March	1907	Traditionally very long and flat, good for sprinters.
Tour of Flanders, Belgium The Ronde	Late March or early April	1913	Lots of sharp climbs up cobbled roads.
Paris–Roubaix, France The Queen of the Classics; the Hell of the North	Early April	1896	A painful journey which covers long stretches of cobbles.
Liège–Bastogne–Liège, Belgium The Grand Old Lady	Late April	1892	A round trip, with long, steep climbs on the return leg.
Giro di Lombardia, Italy Race of the Falling Leaves	September or October	1905	Steep ascents; climbing specialists do well.

The cyclist in front is Eddy Merckx, often described as the greatest cyclist of all time. Between 1966 and 1975 he won each Monument at least twice, as well as 11 Grand Tours.

Stretches of cobbles on the Paris-Roubaix route are graded from 1 (easiest) to 5 (most difficult).

Riding over cobbles is bone-jarring and painful. It's also hard to keep control, especially if the cobbles are dusty, or slippery with rain and mud.

Road bikes

The bikes used for road races are called road bikes. They are designed to be fast on roads, and easy to control through bends.

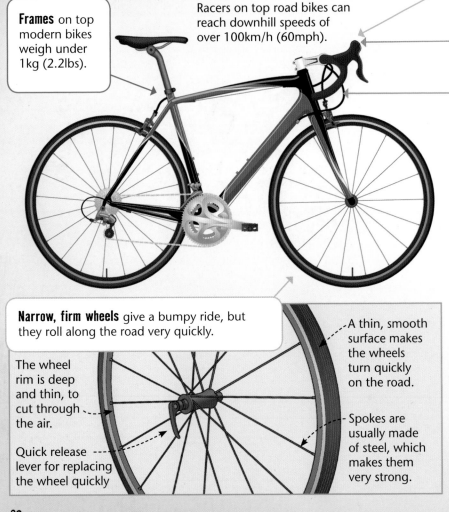

Frames on top modern bikes weigh under 1kg (2.2lbs).

Racers on top road bikes can reach downhill speeds of over 100km/h (60mph).

Narrow, firm wheels give a bumpy ride, but they roll along the road very quickly.

A thin, smooth surface makes the wheels turn quickly on the road.

The wheel rim is deep and thin, to cut through the air.

Quick release lever for replacing the wheel quickly

Spokes are usually made of steel, which makes them very strong.

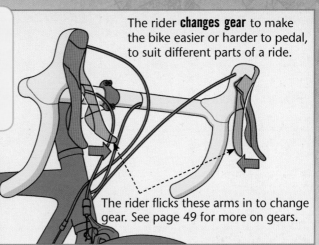

Drop handlebars are curved, and the rider can lean down onto them. This position is great for cutting through air – see page 22.

The gears and brake levers are combined, so the racer has instant access to the controls.

The rider **changes gear** to make the bike easier or harder to pedal, to suit different parts of a ride.

The rider flicks these arms in to change gear. See page 49 for more on gears.

Brakes stop the bike or slow it down. A racing bike has brakes which are lighter and smaller than on many other bikes, so they don't add extra weight.

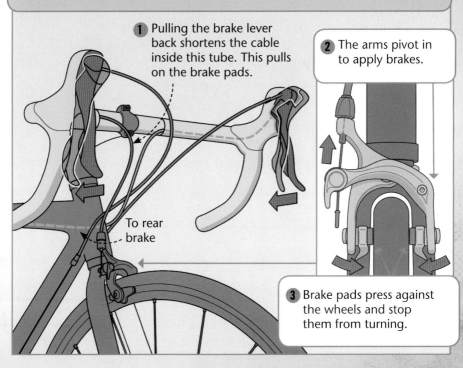

1 Pulling the brake lever back shortens the cable inside this tube. This pulls on the brake pads.

2 The arms pivot in to apply brakes.

To rear brake

3 Brake pads press against the wheels and stop them from turning.

Time trials

Time trials are a type of road race in which riders set off, one by one or in teams, to try to set the fastest time over a given route. They can be stand-alone races, or part of larger stage races such as the Grand Tours.

Saddle is set very high.

This **time trial bike** rider is leaning her body down and forward, so it's as low and narrow as possible. This position helps her to cut through the air and reduce air resistance (see page 10).

Skinsuit is skintight, giving the rider's body a smooth shape.

This special, solid wheel, called a **disc wheel**, cuts through the air very efficiently.

High gearing – lots of teeth on the front cog. See page 49 for more on gears.

Aero helmet is long and smooth, to allow air to pass easily over its surface and help reduce air resistance.

Time trials

- **Length:** usually 20-55km (12-34 miles) – short compared to other professional races
- **Terrain:** largely flat roads
- **Start:** one racer at a time, at set intervals (around a minute)
- **Major events:** UCI World Road Championships, Olympic Games, Grand Tour stages

Rider has arms outstretched on extensions called **aerobars**.

Handlebars are set low.

The **tubes** that make up the bike's frame are a thin oval shape, that cuts through the air efficiently.

Front wheels usually have spokes, as these are easier to steer than disc wheels, which can easily be blown over. Many riders use rear wheels with spokes too, especially in windy conditions.

UCI World Championships

Every year, the UCI holds competitions in all major cycling disciplines. The UCI World Road Championships are a week-long series of road races and time trials. Cyclists compete in national teams for almost all events.

◄---- Mark Cavendish has just won by a fraction of a second, racing on the British team.

These are the final seconds of the men's road race in the 2011 UCI World Road Championships in Copenhagen, Denmark. The location changes every year.

Rainbow jersey

The winner of each UCI Championship is allowed to wear a rainbow jersey in all races in their winning category for the following year.

Over 200 racers competed in the race.

Racing around the world

Road races can take place wherever there's road to be raced on – through baking deserts, snowy mountains and humid tropics.

This map shows some of the biggest road races around the world.

Match the numbers to the table below to see which race is held where.

	Name and country	Month	Race details
1	**Tour Down Under**★, Australia	January	6-day stage race; temperatures can exceed 40°C (104°F)
2	**Tour of San Luis**, Argentina	January	Race over 6 stages and a time trial, with lots of climbs
3	**Tour of Qatar**	February	6-day stage race over flat roads in windy conditions
4	**Tour de Langkawi**, Malaysia	February -March	10-day stage race in humid, hot conditions – around 40°C (104°F)
5	**Tour of California**, USA	May	8-day stage race, including mountain climbs
6	**Tour of Qinghai Lake**, China	July	Race over 13 stages; the route passes a large lake.
7	**USA Pro Cycling Challenge**	August	7-day stage race in the mountainous US state of Colorado
8	**Grand Prix Cycliste de Québec**★ **and de Montréal**★, Canada	September	Day races of laps around a circuit, held 2 days apart in nearby cities

★ Results from the races marked with an ★ are used by the UCI when they calculate world rankings.

This shows the men's Tour of Qatar. A separate Tour for women is held earlier in the month.

This desert Tour is held in February, before temperatures climb too high.

The flat landscape offers little shelter from the wind, so racers form a diagonal paceline called an **echelon** (see page 10 to find out more about pacelines). The leader shelters the others from the wind, and racers take turns at the front.

Para-cycling

Para-cycling competitions are open to atheletes with disabilities, who may use one of the range of cycles shown on these pages.

These tandem riders are racing in the 2008 **Summer Paralympic Games** in Beijing, China. The Paralympics are held after the Olympic Games, every four years.

The **pilot** pedals, steers and works the brakes.

The blind or visually impaired athlete must match the pilot's pedal turns.

Any prizes are jointly awarded to both racers.

The rear handlebars don't turn – they are just for the back rider to lean on.

In this handcycle, the rider lies flat and pushes up. In other designs, the rider sits straight and pushes forwards.

Both handholds move forward together (unlike pedals).

Handcycle (or handbike)

- **How it works:** the racer uses hands and arms to turn handholds, which drive the front wheel (not the rear wheel, as for other bicycles)
- **Used by:** athletes with disabilities that affect their legs or spine
- **Competitions:** road, track and off-road

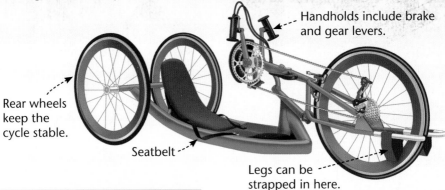

Handholds include brake and gear levers.

Rear wheels keep the cycle stable.

Seatbelt

Legs can be strapped in here.

Tricycle (or trike)

- **How it works:** just like a road bike, but a third wheel makes it much more stable. Many trikes are converted road bikes.
- **Used by:** athletes with disabilities that affect their balance
- **Competitions:** road races

This trike has aerobars, although most trikes have drop handlebars.

Narrow, thin wheels roll smoothly along the road.

The gears sit between the wheels. See page 49 for more about gears.

Gloves help the rider keep a tight grip on the handlebars, even if she has sweaty palms.

These racers are all competing for their national teams. Trade teams do exist in track cycling, but they are less common than in road racing.

These racers are competing in a round of the 2012 UCI Track World Cup. This particular event is a **scratch race**. Read more about scratch races on page 41.

Track races

Track racing is fast and furious. On smooth tracks, racers ride highly specialized bikes in intense, dramatic events which are often won by just fractions of a second.

Velodromes

Track racing takes place on smooth tracks, in arenas called velodromes. Early velodromes were built in many different shapes and sizes, but today, major competitions are held in oval velodromes with steep banks and tight bends.

This velodrome was built in London for the 2012 Olympic Games.

Seating This big velodrome can hold 6,000 spectators.

Sprint start line marks 200m (656ft) to the finish.

Straight sections slope down toward the middle.

Teams set up bases in the central area.

Sprinter's lane where riders may not overtake on the inside

Here, you can see the US women's **pursuit team** at the 2012 Olympic Games, setting a time to qualify for the head-to-head rounds. They went on to win a silver medal. See page 39 for more about pursuit teams.

Velodrome track facts

- **Lap length:** usually 250m (820ft) around the inside of a modern track, though this can vary
- **Surface:** concrete or a road-like surface outdoors; smooth wood or synthetics indoors
- **Major track competitions:** Olympic Games, UCI Track World Championships

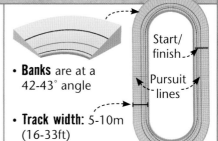

- **Banks** are at a 42-43° angle

- **Track width:** 5-10m (16-33ft)

Start/finish line

Pursuit lines on opposite sides of the track act as start lines for some events. Here they are marked with tape.

Côte d'azur (light blue) warns riders that they are riding so low, they risk clipping a pedal on the steep banks. Here, obstacles help the cyclists to steer clear.

Blue stayer's line separates the track for some races (such as the races on page 41).

Steep-banked curves allow riders to stay on their bikes as they turn the tight bends at high speeds.

33

Sprint races

The fastest track races are called sprint races. Champions are made or broken in dashes that last just seconds.

Track bikes

- **Frame:** rigid, making the bike react fast to pedal turns. Heavier than road bikes.
- **Wheels:** disc, or spoked with deep rims or wide spokes – these are all good at cutting through air

There are no brakes on a track bike, so riders slow down by pushing against the pedals.

This bike is set up for a sprint race. Track bikes for longer events may have aerobars. Those for races with lots of riders may have two spoked wheels, which are slower but easier to control.

Drop handlebars are an ideal shape for pulling on, which helps a racer to pedal hard.

Wheels and pedals are directly linked, so whenever the wheels turn, the pedals turn too.

Five wide spokes

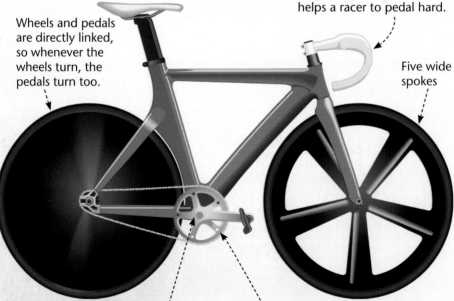

This part of the bike is high, so the pedals don't scrape against the steep sides of the velodrome.

There is just one gear, which is set to suit different racers and events. See page 49 for more on gears.

Track time trials are the fastest sprint events. There are two ways of starting – **standing starts**, which test how quickly a racer can pick up speed; and **flying starts**, for the fastest times of all.

Time trials

- **Competition:** tests of speed
- **Length:** usually 1, 2 or 4 laps
- **Records:** 16.984 seconds for standing start; 9.347 for flying start
- **How to win:** achieve the fastest time

Standing start

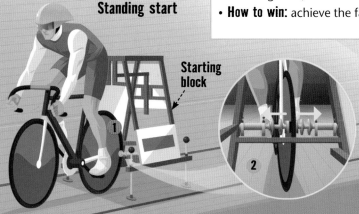

Starting block

1 Just before the race starts, the bike is gripped in a **starting block** (also called a **starting gate**).

2 After 3 beeps, the bike is released. The racer must not turn the pedals before, or the rear wheel spins in the gate, wasting power or even breaking the bike.

3 The timer starts as soon as the bike is released. It will take a few seconds for the racer to reach top speed.

Flying start

1 The racer is pushed onto the track and does a lap at the top, to gather speed and get the bike moving smoothly.

2 The racer swoops down to gather more speed.

Sprint start line

Sprint lane

3 The timer starts when the racer crosses the sprint start line in the sprint lane.

Sprint (or Match Sprint)

- **Format:** Rounds of head-to-head races; usually 2 racers in each
- **Length:** 2 or 3 laps
- **Duration*:** 1-2 minutes, or more if early laps are very slow
- **How to win:** cross the finish line first

Early laps are often slow. Racers may force their opponent to go first, so they can keep an eye on them. But the last lap is always a furious dash to the finish.

Track stand – front rider stops, to force the other rider to overtake.

Team sprint

- **Format:** Rounds of team races
- **Racers on the track:** 2 teams of 2 women or 3 men
- **Start:** from pursuit lines
- **Length:** 2-3 laps
- **Duration:** under 1 minute
- **How to win:** get the final rider of a team across their pursuit line first

1 Teams line up on **pursuit lines**, which are their start/finish lines for this race.

2 Teams form a paceline (see page 10).

3 The leader after each lap leaves the race.

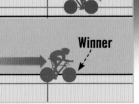

Winner

4 In the final lap, the two remaining contestants sprint to their finish lines.

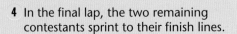

*Race durations shown are approximate lengths of top-level events.

The keirin comes from Japan. It's traditional for spectators to gamble money on who the winner might be.

Keirin

- **Format:** motor-paced group sprint over several rounds
- **Racers on the track:** 6
- **Start:** standing start
- **Length:** 8 laps
- **Duration:** 2-4 minutes
- **How to win:** cross the finish line first

For the first 5.5 laps, racers ride behind a motorized bike, or **derny**, which slowly speeds up. They can't overtake, but can gather speed and jostle for position.

Then, the derny pulls off and the final laps are a sprint to the finish.

Endurance races

The track races on these pages take place over many laps. Success depends on knowing when to hold back, to save energy for a final push to the finish line.

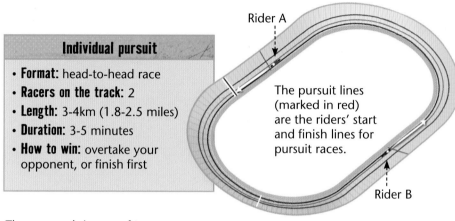

Rider A

Individual pursuit

- **Format:** head-to-head race
- **Racers on the track:** 2
- **Length:** 3-4km (1.8-2.5 miles)
- **Duration:** 3-5 minutes
- **How to win:** overtake your opponent, or finish first

The pursuit lines (marked in red) are the riders' start and finish lines for pursuit races.

Rider B

The race ends in one of two ways:

ENDING 1
If one racer overtakes the other, he or she wins right away.

These racers are using aerobars.

Winner

ENDING 2
If neither racer overtakes the other, then the winner is the first to complete the distance.

Winner

Team pursuit

- **Format:** race between 2 teams of 4
- **Length:** 4km (2.5 miles)
- **Duration:** 30-60 seconds faster than an individual pursuit of the same length
- **How to win:** overtake the other team, or finish first

This is similar to the individual pursuit. But with a team working together, it is an even faster race.

2 He swoops up to let his teammates pass. Then he rejoins them at the back of the paceline to recover.

Team members take turns at the front of the **paceline** (see page 10).

1 This racer has finished his turn at the front.

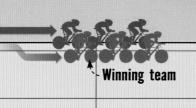

Only three riders need to make it to the finish line. The fourth rider often works extra hard to lead the team, then drops out, exhausted.

The race ends in one of two ways:

Winning team

Riders often 'bunch up' at the finish.

Winning team

ENDING 1
If the 3rd racer of one team overtakes the 3rd racer of the other team, the faster team wins.

ENDING 2
If neither team overtakes the other, each team's finishing time is that of their 3rd rider. The fastest team wins.

Starting positions

The races on these pages start with a **mass rolling start**. Racers begin from two lines, along the track sides. The first lap doesn't count – it lets them merge into a group.

Half of the riders line up in the sprinter's lane. Their bikes are held upright by helpers.

The other half line up holding onto the rail.

1 Every second lap is a sprint. The racer who crosses the line last leaves the race. The other laps don't count.

Elimination race

Also called 'Devil Scratch Race', or 'Devil Takes the Hindmost'
- **Racers on the track:** 18-24
- **Duration:** 10-12 minutes
- **How to win:** be the last racer remaining at the end

2 The losing rider's number is called out; or, for top races, a light flashes red on their handlebars.

3 The final lap is a sprint between the two remaining racers.

Racers are eliminated one by one.

Madison

- **Racers on the track:** up to 30. Each rider on the track is part of a 2-person team, who take turns to race.
- **Length:** up to 50km (31 miles); 25km (15.5 miles) for UCI competitions
- **How to win:** ride the most laps in a set time, or be first to cover a set length
- **Duration:** varies depending on distance – often an hour or more

Rider A is taking over from Rider B, using a technique called a **handsling**.

Rider A

Rider B

1 Rider A moves below the stayer's line (see page 33).

2 Rider B takes rider A's hand and hurls him into the race.

3 Rider B moves above the stayer's line and cycles slowly until it's his turn again.

Points race

- **Racers on the track:** around 20
- **Length:** 20-30km (12-19 miles)
- **Duration:** 25-40 minutes
- **How to win:** win the most points

- **Points:** racers are awarded points for where they're placed in a series of sprints throughout the race.

1st place in each sprint lap = 5   2nd = 3   3rd = 2   4th = 1

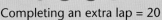

Completing an extra lap = 20

Scratch race

- **Racers on the track:** up to 24
- **Length:** 10-15km (6-9 miles)
- **Duration:** 15-18 minutes
- **How to win:** be first to the finish

A long-distance race to the finish line, with no points or sprint laps.

The first ever six-day race was held in London in 1878. In early six-day races, riders worked alone and barely took a break – many became ill from the effort.

Racers can cover over 100km (62 miles) on each night of the event.

Late-night races

Some track meetings are held at night, with loud music, disco lights and crowds of cheering spectators enjoying a night out. The most famous of these events are **six-day races**.

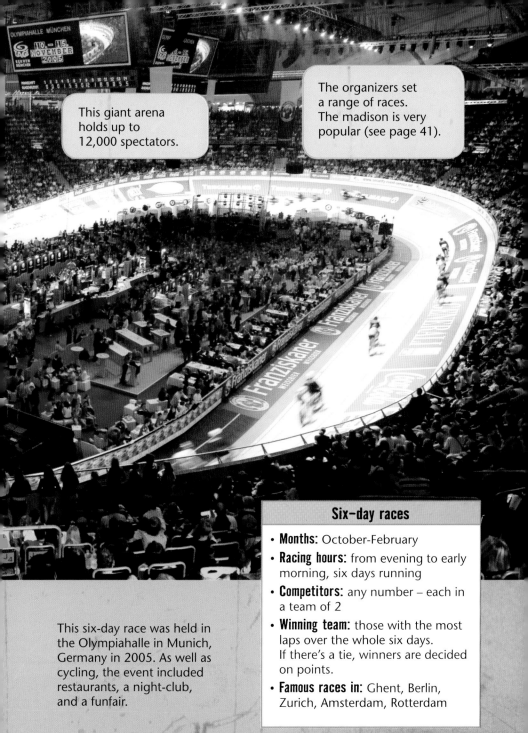

This giant arena holds up to 12,000 spectators.

The organizers set a range of races. The madison is very popular (see page 41).

This six-day race was held in the Olympiahalle in Munich, Germany in 2005. As well as cycling, the event included restaurants, a night-club, and a funfair.

Six-day races

- **Months:** October-February
- **Racing hours:** from evening to early morning, six days running
- **Competitors:** any number – each in a team of 2
- **Winning team:** those with the most laps over the whole six days. If there's a tie, winners are decided on points.
- **Famous races in:** Ghent, Berlin, Zurich, Amsterdam, Rotterdam

The Hour Record

The UCI Hour Record challenges riders to cycle as far as they can on a track in an hour. It's an extreme test of strength and stamina – one of the toughest in cycling.

The first hour record of 25.5km (15.8 miles) was set by **Frank Dodd** on a 'penny farthing' bike in **1876**.

In **1893**, **Henri Desgrange** (see page 17) cycled 35.32km (21.95 miles) in an hour. This was the first record recognized by the cycling organization that became the UCI.

Over the decades, cyclists set a series of new records. They included **Fausto Coppi** (45.871km (28.50 miles)) and **Jacques Anquetil** (46.159km (28.68 miles)) who both went on to become Grand Tour champions (see pages 12-16).

Fausto Coppi

Wire spokes

In **1972**, cycling legend **Eddy Merckx** set a new record of 49.43km (30.7 miles). He called it, 'the hardest ride I've ever done'.

Merckx held the record for 12 years. Then, new techniques and bike designs led to a string of new records. Here are some of them.

Disc wheels

1984: 51.151km (31.78 miles)

Set by **Francesco Moser** using disc wheels (see page 22).

'Praying Mantis' position

1993: 51.596km (32.06 miles)
1994: 52.713km (32.75 miles)

Set by **Graeme Obree**. He invented new positions, including the 'Praying Mantis'.

In 1996, Boardman used a new position invented by Obree, called the 'Superman'.

1993: 52.27km (32.48 miles)
1996: 56.375km (35.03 miles)

Set by **Chris Boardman**.

In the late 1990s, the UCI decreed that records could only be set using the equipment that Merckx had used. All records after 1972 were downgraded.

In October **2000**, **Chris Boardman** broke Merckx's record under the new rules by just 10m (33ft).

In **2014** the UCI altered the rules again, to allow modern track equipment. Many top racers will now attempt to set records under these new rules.

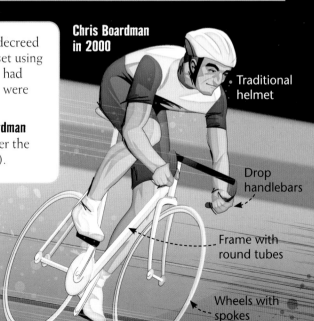

Chris Boardman in 2000

Traditional helmet

Drop handlebars

Frame with round tubes

Wheels with spokes

MTB

MTB (mountain biking) takes place over challenging terrain, such as steep climbs and descents, jumps, and stony or muddy paths.

Here, Canadian racer Steve Smith is competing in a DH (downhill) race at Crankworx, a 10-day MTB festival held every year in Whistler, Canada.

Hardy bikes

Mountain bikes are built to withstand tough, off-road conditions.

Mountain bike

- **Frame:** strong material such as steel, titanium or carbon. They are heavier and sturdier than road bikes.
- **Wheels:** wide – up to 6.5cm (2.5in) across to help the rider to balance, with thick tread for gripping muddy or wet ground
- **Gears:** lots – usually 18-30 – to cope with a wide range of off-road terrain

A **suspension fork** lessens the impact when a bike hits obstacles or lands after a jump. The front wheel's movement is absorbed, so the handlebars aren't jarred.

The **stanchions** contain an air chamber or coil springs.

When the bike hits an obstacle, the stanchions move down, and absorb the impact.

Below is a **hardtail** mountain bike, which has suspension at the front. Most mountain bikes are hardtails.

See page 54 for a bike with both front and rear suspension.

Flat, wide handlebars give the rider a strong, stable position.

These are **disc brakes** – great for riding in mud.

Pedal power

In all bikes, power from turning the pedals is used to drive the rear wheel using a chain and **sprockets** – metal cogs with teeth.

Chain is hooked onto one of the rear **sprockets**.

How it works

1 Pushing on the **pedals** turns the **crank**, which turns the sprockets at the front.

2 The **chain** is hooked onto the metal teeth of a front sprocket, so it turns as well.

3 The chain is also hooked onto a rear sprocket, which turns too. This turning drives the rear wheel.

Crank Pedal

Derailleurs are devices that move the chain from sprocket to sprocket.

Chain

Chain is hooked onto one of the front **sprockets**.

Gears

Changing gear is when you switch the chain onto different-sized sprockets, to make the bike easier or harder to pedal. This is useful when changing terrain.

This picture shows a bike in a **high gear**, which is ideal for smooth flat roads.	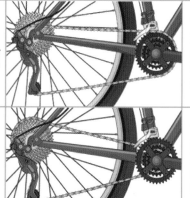	The chain is on the largest front sprocket and the smallest rear sprocket. It's harder to pedal but you travel further with each turn.
This picture shows a bike in a **low gear**, which is ideal for climbs.		The chain is on the smallest front sprocket and the largest rear spocket. You don't go so far with each turn, but it's easier to pedal.

49

XC (Cross-Country)

XC (cross-country) races are fast-paced dashes across rocky terrain and up steep climbs.

The racers wait in a group. Suddenly the klaxon sounds, and they're off.

Racers battle to get close to the front...

... ready for the first **singletrack** – a narrow route, where they'll be forced to ride single-file.

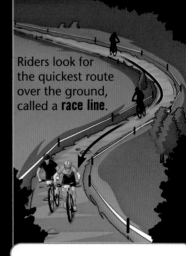

Riders look for the quickest route over the ground, called a **race line**.

Riders can only overtake when the route gets wider again.

Sometimes the route hits obstacles – such as boulders or jumps – and splits into two.

The longer route – slower but with no obstacles – is often called the **chicken run**.

This shorter route includes a jump. It's quicker but more risky.

Racers pace themselves over steep **climbs**.

Coming **downhill** requires extreme concentration and great bike handling skills – it's easy to lose control and fall.

Sitting in the saddle saves energy.

Standing is more strenuous, but gives the rider more power to pedal.

By the end, racers are usually spread out over the course. The winner is the first over the finish line.

Long-distance riding

MTB long-distance events include marathon XC races over rugged terrain, MTB stage races, long trails running from the tops of towering mountains, and races that run all through the night.

Long-distance MTB racing		
Event	**Competition**	**Major events**
24-hour races	Racers compete to ride the most laps over 24 hours – either solo, or in teams with members taking turns to ride.	Mountain Mayhem (UK), Sleepless in the Saddle (UK, USA, Australia), 24 Hours of Adrenalin (USA, Canada)
Enduro (or All-Mountain)	Racers are timed over several downhill stages, and must also cycle between stages. Courses are usually around 30-50km (19-31 miles) long.	Enduro World Series (held all around the world), Bluegrass Enduro Tour (Europe), North American Enduro Tour (USA)
Marathon	A long cross-country race. UCI-organized marathons are between 60-160 km (37-100 miles) long; other marathons can be much longer.	UCI Mountain Bike Marathon World Championships, Megavalanche (downhill marathon in France)
Stage race	Up to 8 stages raced on consecutive days, solo or in teams. Some stage races also include a time trial.	Asba Cape Epic (South Africa), TransAlps (Europe), La Ruta de los Conquistadores (Costa Rica)

This photo shows the Cape Epic stage
race in South Africa, often known as
the mountain biking equivalent
to the Tour de France. It covers
over 700km (435 miles)
over 8 days each year.

MTB DH (Downhill)

DH (downhill) races are short and intense. From a high point, racers hurl themselves down a steep descent, over jumps, drops and uneven ground, and around sharp bends.

Downhill bikes are heavy but sturdy, built for speed on incredibly tough terrain. They are difficult to ride uphill, and riders often get them towed up to the start of the course.

1. Wide, high handlebars let the rider shift his weight back, to control descents.

2. Shock absorbers at the front and rear give **full suspension**.

3. Full-face helmet, goggles, full-finger gloves and body padding

4. Small, fat wheels make the bike stable. They have a thick tread, to grip the terrain, whether muddy, dusty or hard.

Some DH events are held in hilly cities, such as this 2012 race in La Paz, Bolivia. Racers fly down narrow streets, roads and stairs, and jump over huts, buildings and specially built ramps.

Downhill race facts

- **Race length:** 1.5-3.5km (1-2 miles)
- **Winning time:** 1-5 minutes
- **Start:** individual starts from the course top
- **Terrain:** downhill track with lots of obstacles and jumps
- **Major events:** UCI Mountain Bike World Cup, Crankworx (Whistler, Canada), Sea Otter Classic (California, USA)

This DH rider is stretched low over his bike, in a stable position that helps him balance and control the descent.

4X (Four cross)

4X races have up to four riders going head-to-head over a short downhill course in a frantic race to the finish. Courses twist over jumps and around steeply banked curves called berms. Races are swift and action-packed, and crashes are common.

This is a round of the 2010 4X World Cup, held in Fort William, Scotland.

Bikes are strong and tough, with front or full suspension.

The numberplate identifies the rider. Often the number is the rider's qualifying position (see opposite).

Full-face helmet protects the rider's face if he crashes, and keeps dust out of his eyes.

Obstacles such as jumps, logs or rocks are common.

Four cross (4X)

- **Length:** around 500m (0.3 miles)
- **Winning time:** 30-60 seconds
- **Terrain:** a short, downhill course over dirt, with jumps and berms
- **Racers:** 3-4 racers in each race; total number competing varies
- **Major events:** 4X Pro-Tour Circuit

Knock-out competitions

4X competitions are made up of rounds of races. Winners go through to the next round; losers have to leave. Here's how it works:

Qualification
Riders set a time over the course. They are ranked in order of speed, and the fastest qualify for the heats.

Knock-out rounds
All qualifiers race in the first rounds, in groups of 3 or 4. 2 winners from each race go through to the next round. The rest are knocked out.

Finals
Once there are just 4 competitiors remaining, they have a final race to be champion.

Trials

In MTB trials, competitors put their balance and bike-handling skills to the test to overcome a series of obstacles, without putting their feet down.

Track stand Rider sits on the bike, with the front wheel at an angle to help balance.

Rider may **take a dab** (put a foot down) at a particularly difficult section, taking a point rather than risk falling.

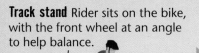

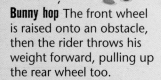

Bunny hop The front wheel is raised onto an obstacle, then the rider throws his weight forward, pulling up the rear wheel too.

Drop off Rider jumps to the ground, usually rear wheel first.

Penalty points		
Each section is scored out of 5. A **clean** score of 0 is best. If a rider reaches 5 before finishing, they quit the section and move on to the next one.		
1 point	Every time a foot, or other body or bike part (other than the wheels) is used for balance.	
	Every 15 seconds if the rider goes over the time limit (usually 2 minutes, 30 seconds).	
5 points	Falling off, or if a hand or both feet touch the ground.	
	Going out of the course boundaries (marked by tape and arrows).	

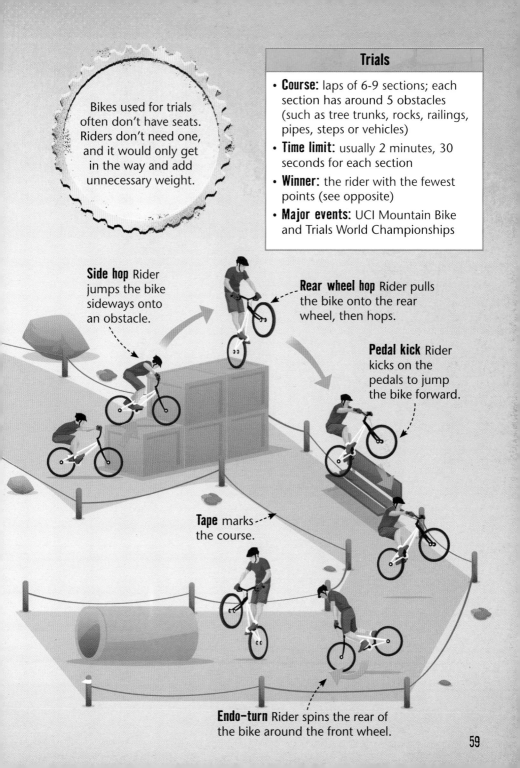

Bikes used for trials often don't have seats. Riders don't need one, and it would only get in the way and add unnecessary weight.

Trials

- **Course:** laps of 6-9 sections; each section has around 5 obstacles (such as tree trunks, rocks, railings, pipes, steps or vehicles)
- **Time limit:** usually 2 minutes, 30 seconds for each section
- **Winner:** the rider with the fewest points (see opposite)
- **Major events:** UCI Mountain Bike and Trials World Championships

Side hop Rider jumps the bike sideways onto an obstacle.

Rear wheel hop Rider pulls the bike onto the rear wheel, then hops.

Pedal kick Rider kicks on the pedals to jump the bike forward.

Tape marks the course.

Endo-turn Rider spins the rear of the bike around the front wheel.

Portage

Racers may carry their bikes over very slippery or steep patches. This is called *portage*, from the French word *porter*, 'to carry'.

CX

CX (cyclo-cross) racers navigate their road-style bikes over laps of off-road terrain in winter. They may face snow and ice, or fields of deep mud.

Cyclo-cross facts

- **Time:** 1 hour or under
- **Circuit:** 2.5-3.5km (1.5-2 miles) long
- **Winner:** the first racer to complete the distance, made up of a set number of laps
- **Months:** October-February
- **Major events:** Super Prestige series, UCI Cyclo-Cross World Championships

---

CX bikes

CX bikes look like road bikes, but with adaptations.

This 'triangle' frame fits over a shoulder, so the bike can be easily carried.

Wide handlebars give the rider a stable position.

Wide bumpy wheels, to grip mud or snow

Unlike standard road bike brakes (see page 21), these brakes sit below the wheel's rim. This means that they're less likely to get clogged up with mud from the wheels.

BMX

In the 1970s, young American cyclists started riding on off-road tracks originally built for motorcycle racing. Today, BMX (bicycle motocross) is hugely popular. It covers everything from freestyle tricks in skateparks and on city streets, to high-speed races.

Here are BMX racers at the BMX Supercross World Cup, in Denmark in 2009. Falls are common, so riders wear protective clothing.

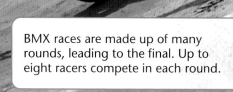

BMX races are made up of many rounds, leading to the final. Up to eight racers compete in each round.

Full-face helmet and goggles

Protective gloves

The best riders keep their speed constant, even over bumps and through bends.

BMX racing bikes are built to go quickly over jumps and around banked curves. They have long, light frames.

BMX freestyle bikes have a similar shape, but they are shorter and sturdier, which helps to do tricks.

BMX racing bike

Lightweight tubes

Low seat

Wide handlebars

Small wheels

Single gear

BMX racing

BMX races are short, intense races over bumps, jumps and berms (steep-sided banks). Racers need speed, strength and superb bike control.

BMX race facts

- **Length:** around 350m (1,150ft)
- **Track:** smooth tarmac or dirt, over bumps and around berms
- **Riders on the track:** up to 8
- **Winning time:** around 40 seconds
- **Major events:** Olympic Games, UCI BMX Supercross World Cup and Championships

This diagram shows an example of a BMX track.

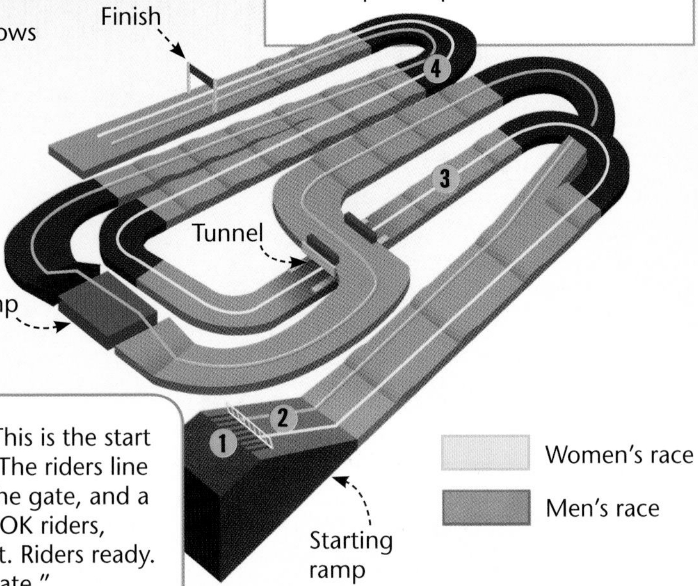

Finish

Tunnel

Jump

Starting ramp

Women's race

Men's race

1 Gate start This is the start to the race. The riders line up against the gate, and a voice says, "OK riders, random start. Riders ready. Watch the gate."

Gate

2 Ramp A few seconds later, the gate drops. The racers sprint forwards, down the **ramp**.

3 Rhythm section is a series of low bumps or jumps. Here are some of the techniques a BMX rider can use to cover them.

Pumping – the rider pumps up and down to propel the bike smoothly over the bumps.

Weight forwards, arms bent

Weight back

Jump – both wheels lift off the ground.

Manual – the rider lifts the front wheel, and pedals along on the rear wheel.

4 Berms (steep-sided banks) Riders lean into them so they don't lose their balance and their outside pedals don't scrape the ground.

Racers stop turning the pedals as they start to turn.

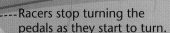

This rider may try to overtake by coming down on the inside of the bend.

The leader swoops down as he exits the berm, to increase his speed.

Riders start turning the pedals again as they exit the berm.

BMX: Freestyle

BMX freestyle is all about stunts, called **tricks**. Riders are judged on the complexity of their tricks and how well they perform them. They may also be scored on how well they link them together.

There are five kinds of freestyle: dirt, park, street, vert and flatland.

Dirt bikes are the toughest BMX bikes, with strong frames and wheels. They look a little like mountain bikes – and some dirt jumpers do use mountain bikes instead.

This BMX rider holds onto his saddle with both hands as he performs dirt jumping in Wanaka, New Zealand. This trick is called a **double seat grab superman**.

Often two dirt mounds are built close together with a gap in between – called a 'double'.

Mound 1

Mound 2

BMX Dirt

Dirt riders jump high over mounds of compressed earth or sand, and perform amazing tricks in the air.

- **Competitions**: Riders perform 3 jumps, scored by judges
- **Major events**: Red Bull Empire of Dirt

This BMX vert rider is competing at the Summer X Games in California, USA, in 2009.

Tuck no hander Handlebars are pulled into the body, and arms are stretched out.

BMX Vert

Vert (short for vertical) riders perform air tricks in u-shaped ramps – often with very high sides. They pick up speed, then do tricks mid-air.

- **Competitions**: a series of tricks lasting up to 40 seconds, scored by experts
- **Major events**: X Games, BMX Big Air

BMX Park

Park riders perform a range of air- and land-based tricks on obstacles in skateparks or specially built BMX parks.

- **Competitions**: runs of up to 40 seconds, scored by experts
- **Major events**: X Games, X Fest, Dew Tour

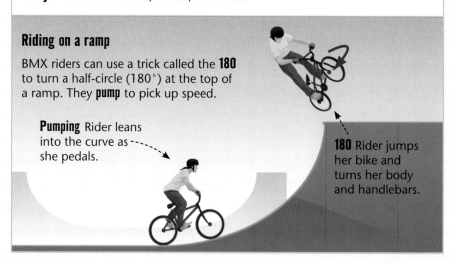

Riding on a ramp

BMX riders can use a trick called the **180** to turn a half-circle (180°) at the top of a ramp. They **pump** to pick up speed.

Pumping Rider leans into the curve as she pedals.

180 Rider jumps her bike and turns her body and handlebars.

Here are some popular **air tricks** – performed mid-air on vert ramps, dirt jumps and in skateparks. More air tricks are being invented all the time.

Backflip Bike and rider flip backwards in a complete circle.

Tailwhip Bike is kicked in a complete spin around the handlebars.

Superman Legs are held away from the pedals, and rider's body is held straight.

This trick is called a **grind**. It uses **pegs** on the wheels to slide down the railing.

Pegs

BMX Street

Street riders perform tricks in towns and city streets. They work urban obstacles such as stairs, railings and walls into their runs.

- **Competitions:** runs of up to 45 seconds, scored by experts
- **Major events:** X Games, X Fest, Dew Tour

BMX Flatland

Flatlanders perform tricks on a hard, flat surface. A run is based purely on the rider and his or her bike. Here are some examples of flatland tricks.

- **Competitions:** several runs lasting for a set length of time, e.g. 2 minutes
- **Major events:** Flatland World Circuit, Red Bull Flatland Voodoo Jam

Pogo Rider pulls her bike upright, stands on the pegs and hops on the rear wheel.

Hang 5 Rider puts one foot on the front peg; the other is used to balance.

This flatlander is performing a trick called a **cross footed nose wheelie**.

Other events

Team sports, gymnastics, dancing – many different activities are possible on a bike. Here are a few other events that fall outside of the usual cycling disciplines.

Unicycling

A unicycle has just one wheel, and requires great balance. Many unicyclists perform tricks – whether as part of a routine, or navigating a trials course.

MUni, or mountain unicycling, involves riding a hardy unicycle over rocks and trails.

Arm stretched out for balance

Artistic cycling

Cyclists perform a routine to music. They often work in teams, and moves can include lifts, handstands and headstands.

Ball sports

Ball sports are played
in teams on bikes.

Plastic disc to protect
spokes from the ball

Bike polo is a fast-paced
sport that's becoming
especially popular in
cities, where it's played
on hard courts.

Bike polo

Two teams battle to score goals by hitting a
ball into a goal using mallets.

- **Players:** 3 per team on a hard court, 4 or 5
  on grass
- **Game duration:** either a set time limit (usually
  10-15 minutes), or until 5 goals are scored
- **Major competition:** World Hardcourt Bike
  Polo Championships

Everyday bikes

For millions around the world, cycling is a way of getting around – to and from work, around busy city streets or to explore new places. There's a range of bikes, to suit every situation.

Hybrid bike

Hybrids come in many styles. The most popular is a cross between a road bike and a MTB, with no suspension. These bikes are great for riding on roads, grass and country tracks.

- **Ideal for:** city cyclists using busy roads; cyclists of all ages and abilities

Electric bikes can be powered at least partly by electric motors, for an easier ride. They are especially popular with commuters, and riders with health problems.

Light frame and wheels, so it's fast and easy to pedal.

Flat handlebars give an upright position, safer for watching out on busy roads.

Mudguard stops mud from flying up onto the rider.

Touring bike

Similar to a road bike, but more comfortable, with fatter wheels and a more upright position. Panniers at the front and back allow plenty of baggage to be carried.

- **Ideal for:** tourists on a cycling tour

Drop handlebars allow the rider to change position from time to time on a long ride.

A rider can lean on the hoods...

... or on the drops.

Panniers can go at the front and back.

Folding bike

A small-wheeled bike that folds up into an easy-to-transport package. Some are very basic; others have many gears and full suspension.

- **Ideal for:** commuters who need to catch a busy train or bus on their journey to work; people without much storage space at home

Handlebars and seat are at normal heights.

Long seat post can be lowered.

Rear wheel section can unlock to swing in.

To fold, the wheels swing in, the seat post lowers, and the handlebars rotate down.

The bike folds in around these hinges.

Glossary

This glossary explains some of the words used in this book. If a word is written in *italic* type, it has an entry of its own.

aerobars Extensions on handlebars that allow a racer to lean forward. They are often used in *time trials*.

air resistance The pushing of air against a moving object, slowing it down.

berm A steep-sided bend.

BMX Bicycle motocross – a type of cycling that started in the 1970s when children copied motorcycle racing.

BMX freestyle Using *BMX* bikes to perform tricks and jumps.

BMX racing Using *BMX* bikes to race around a short course with jumps, bumps and *berms*.

breakaway Any racer or group who breaks away to race ahead of the *peloton*.

crank The lever that attaches the pedals to the front *sprocket*. The motion of the pedals turns the crank, which ultimately makes the wheels turn around.

CX (cyclo–cross) A race over laps of a *XC* course in winter months.

DH (downhill) A race in which riders set off at intervals from a high starting point down to the finish, over a rough course. The rider with the fastest time wins.

discipline A sub-category of a sport that has its own set of rules and events.

disc wheel A solid wheel (or one with covers fitted over the spokes).

echelon A diagonal *paceline*, used when there's a strong side wind blowing.

endurance event A type of event that takes place over a long time and distance, requiring stamina.

gear A system of *sprockets* and a chain that, using pedal power, propels the bike. On many bikes it's possible to change gear, to make it easier or harder to pedal.

Grand Tours The three biggest, best-known *stage races*.

hardtail A mountain bike with front *suspension* but none at the rear.

mass start A race start where all racers set off together at the same time.

MTB (mountain biking) The sport of riding a mountain bike, off-road, over courses that often involve jumps, obstacles and uneven ground.

paceline A group of cyclists working together to overcome *air resistance*. The front rider pushes aside air, and the others follow in the *slipstream*. Riders take turns to go at the front.

park A purpose-built area with obstacles where *BMX freestyle* riders perform *tricks*.

peloton The group formed by the majority of racers in a road race.

pursuit A race where two racers or teams chase each other around a track.

race line The path a rider chooses over the ground, to give the quickest or easiest route.

rhythm section A series of small bumps in a *BMX race* course.

run A routine made up of a set number of *tricks* in *BMX freestyle* events.

singletrack A narrow path on a *XC* course where racers have to ride single-file.

slipstream An area behind a moving cyclist where *air resistance* is reduced.

spokes Thin metal rods connecting the middle of the wheel to its outside.

sprint event A type of track event that is short and fast-paced.

sprocket A metal cog that makes up part of the *gears*.

stage race A cycling race that takes place over several days or weeks, made up of a series of day races called stages.

street A *discipline* where *tricks* are performed on obstacles you might find in a street, such as handrails.

suspension Part of a bike that dampens shocks and jolts to give a smooth ride.

time trial A race against the clock where riders set off to cover a set course as fast as they can. The rider or team with the fastest time wins.

track cycling Cycling which takes place on a smooth track, usually in a *velodrome*. It is often fast-paced.

tread The patterns of grooves in a bike wheel to improve grip.

trials A *MTB discipline* which involves riders navigating a course of obstacles without stepping on the ground.

trick A stunt, such as a flip, done in *BMX freestyle* events.

UCI The Union Cycliste Internationale, the world's cycling body based in Switzerland, which sets cycling rules, admininsters penalties, calculates world rankings and organizes some races.

UCI World Championships International events held by the *UCI* in the main cycling *disciplines*.

velodrome An arena containing an oval cycling track with steeply banked curves at either end, and places for spectators to watch.

vert ramp A u-shaped ramp used in *BMX freestyle*.

XC (cross-country) A *MTB* race over an off-road course, often including jumps, obstacles and climbs.

Index

Cycling on the internet

For links to websites where you can find out more about the different kinds of cycling, watch videos of professional cyclists, races and competitions, and discover how you can get involved, go to the Usborne Quicklinks website at **www.usborne.com/quicklinks** and enter the keyword: **cycling**

Please follow the internet safety Guidelines at the Usborne Quicklinks website.

Acknowledgements

Every effort has been made to trace and acknowledge ownership of copyright. If any rights have been omitted, the publishers offer to rectify this in any future editions following notification. The publishers are grateful to the following individuals and organizations for permission to reproduce material on the following pages:

cover © Larry Clouse/ZUMA Press/Corbis; **p1** © Jose Miguel Gomez/ Reuters/Corbis; **p2-3** © Kolesky/Nikon/Lexar; **p4-5** © Allan McKenzie/ SWpix.com; **p6** © epa european pressphoto agency b.v./Alamy; **p7** © Josh McElwee; **p8-9** © Cathal McNaughton/Reuters/Corbis; **p10-11** © Jean-Christophe Bott/epa/Corbis; **p12** Bryn Lennon/Getty Images; **p14a-15a** © Simon Wilkinson/SWpix.com; **p16** © Offside - L'Equipe; **p18-19** © Offside - L'Equipe; **p22-23** © Mick Tsikas/Reuters/Corbis; **p24-25** Jonathan Nackstrand/AFP/Getty Images; **p26-27** © Tim de Waele/TDWsport.com/ Corbis; **p28** © Feng Li/Getty Images; **p30-31** © Leo Mason/Corbis; **p32-33** © Tim Clayton/Corbis; **p37** Mike Hewitt/Getty Images; **p42-43** © Stefan Obermeier/Robert Harding; **p46-47** Fraser Britton/Mountain Biking UK Magazine via Getty Images; **p52-53** © Karin Schermbrucker (www. slingshotmedia.co.za); **p54-55** © David Mercado/Reuters/Corbis; **p56-57** © Kenny Ferguson/Alamy; **p60-61** © TDWsport/Corbis; **p62-63** © imageBROKER/Alamy; **p66-67** © Miles Holden Photography; **p68** Christian Pondella/Getty Images; **p71** © Josh McElwee; **p72** © Harrison Shull/Robert Harding; **p73** © Piero Cruciatti/Alamy

Bicycle illustrations by Tim from KJA Artists
Additional design and illustration by Alice Reece
Series editor: Jane Chisholm   Series designer: Zoe Wray
Digital design by John Russell   Picture research by Ruth King